Lee's

EXCELLENT
ENGLISH

BEGINNER COURSE

Lesson 1 - 25

Ukrainian Edition

Lee's Books

Copyright © 2021 Lee's Books
All rights reserved.

ISBN: 9798792339583

This book belongs to

_____

Contents

Lesson
1
- Learn the words
- Learn the sentences
- Learn the phonics
- Test yourself!

My pencil case

мій пенал

Learn the words

1. a pencil
олівець

2. an eraser
гумка

3. some glue
клей

4. a pencil sharpener
точилка

5. some whiteout
коректор

6. a pen
ручка

7. a ruler
лінійка

8. some tape
сантиметр

9. a marker
маркер

10. a crayon
кольоровий олівець

Write the missing letters!

1. p_ _c_ _

2. e_a_e_

3. g_ _ _

4. pe_c_l sh_r_ _n_ _

5. w_i_ _o_t

6. p_ _

7. r_ _ _r

8. t_ _ _

9. m_r_e_

10. c_a_o_

Have fun with the words!

Word Search

```
c e z c a p n g y j c t x m e m h k
z l y r r e m s d r d m a r k e r q
h u n a h n h h f i k i f v x u l j
u n w y p e n c i l e a j s n d o y
x q d o g c e r a s e r x b x a i o
f b h n w t n g w h i t e o u t h e
u o c v g t a k h c s r x v a h q y
f v u x l p c p v i g u u x m u q g
r c s c u a w f e b e l j d r o c x
z e p b e o j p k d p e b a z r h e
t c b y h a l k d k v r f z o a f l
w a p e n c i l s h a r p e n e r v
```

Words are hidden → ↓ and ↘.

pencil sharpener	**pen**
marker	**whiteout**
crayon	**ruler**
tape	**glue**
pencil	**eraser**

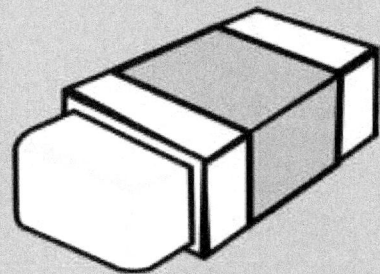

What is this?

It is <u>a pencil</u>.

It is not <u>an eraser</u>.

What is that?

It is <u>a crayon</u>.

It is not <u>a marker</u>.

Write the missing words!

What _____ this?

It is a _____ sharpener.

It is _____ a _____ .

What _____ _____ ?

_____ is an _____ .

It _____ a _____ .

What _____ this?

It _____ a _____ .

_____ is _____ .

_____ ?

_____ .

_____ .

Is this a <u>marker</u>?   Is that <u>whiteout</u>?

Yes, it is.   Yes, it is.

No, it is not.   No, it is not.

Write the missing words!

Is this a _____?

Yes, it _____.

No, _____ is _____.

Is this _____ _____?

_____, it _____.

_____, it is _____.

Is _____ a _____?

Yes, _____ _____.

No, _____ _____.

_____?

_____.

_____.

a /æ/

cat /kæt/

fan /fæn/

sad /sæd/

hat /hæt/

More words

has

bad

dad

bag

apple

Write the words

a /æ/

Write the letters & Read the sentences!

My d_d h_s a s_d c_t.

This h_t is b_d.

The _pple is in the b_g.

Complete the words

1. p_____l   3. m_____r   5. c_____n

2. t_____e   4. e_____r   6. w_____t

Write the answer next to the letter "A"

A: ___ **7.** ___ is ___ eraser.

a. This, a
b. they, an
c. It, an

A: ___ **8.** It ___ not a ___.

a. is, eraser
b. is, pencil sharpener
c. are, marker

A: ___ **9.** What is this? It is ___ tape.

a. a
b. an
c. x

A: ___ **10.** Is this ___? No, it ___.

a. pencil, is not
b. tape, is not
c. whiteout, not

Answers on Page 156

Lesson 2

- Learn the words
- Learn the sentences
- Learn the phonics
- Test yourself!

In the classroom

в класі

Learn the words

1. **chair**
стілець

2. **desk**
стіл

3. **blackboard**
класна дошка

4. **whiteboard**
біла дошка

5. **computer**
комп'ютер

6. **globe**
глобус

7. **clock**
годинник

8. **book**
книга

9. **bookshelf**
книжкова полиця

10. **poster**
плакат

Write the missing letters!

1. c_ _ _r

2. d_ _ _

3. bl_c_b_a_ _

4. w_it_b_a_d

5. _o_p_t_r

6. g_ _ _e

7. cl_c_

8. b_ _k

9. b_o_sh_l_

10. p_s_e_

Have fun with the words!

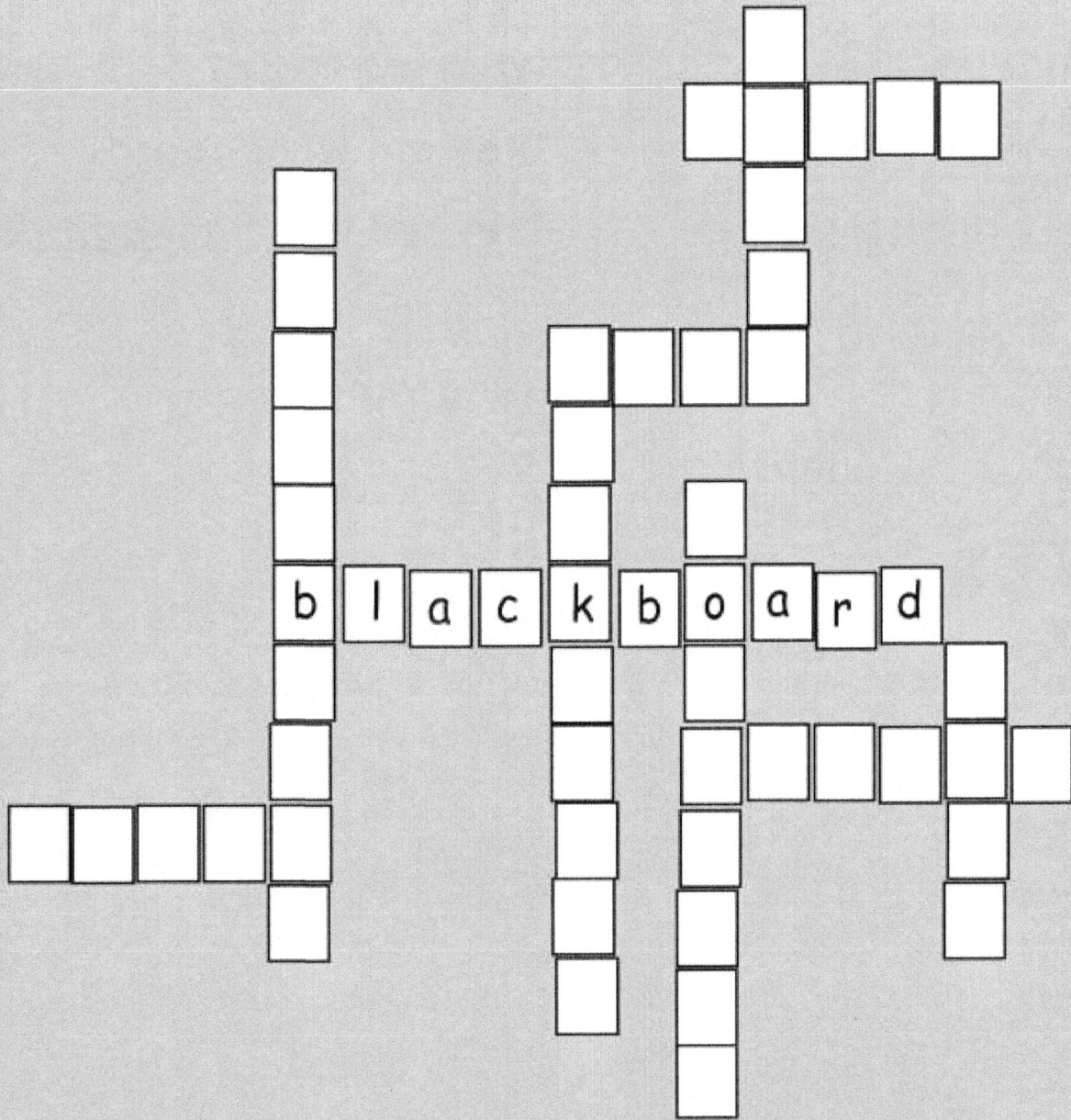

b l a c k b o a r d

1. desk
2. blackboard
3. computer
4. bookshelf
5. clock
6. whiteboard
7. poster
8. book
9. globe
10. chair

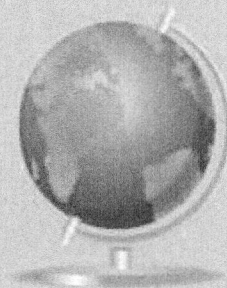

What are these?   What are those?

They are <u>chair</u>s.   They are <u>whiteboard</u>s.

They are not <u>desk</u>s.   They are not <u>blackboard</u>s.

Write the missing words!

What _____ these?

They are _____.

They _____ _____ bookshelves.

What _____ those?

They _____ _____.

They are _____ _____.

What _____ _____?

_____ are _____.

_____ _____ not _____.

_____?

_____.

_____.

Are these <u>globes</u>?

Yes, they are.

No, they are not.

Are those <u>computers</u>?

Yes, they are.

No, they are not.

Write the missing words!

Are these _____ ?

Yes, they _____ .

No, _____ are _____ .

Are those _____ ?

_____ , they _____ .

_____ , they are _____ .

_____ these _____ ?

Yes, _____ _____ .

No, _____ _____ _____ .

_____ ?

_____ .

_____ .

e /ɛ/

pen /pɛn/

bed /bɛd/

leg /lɛg/

10

ten /tɛn/

More words

met

get

hen

red

tent

Write the words

e /ɛ/

Write the letters & Read the sentences!

I will g_t a r_d p_n.

I see t_n h_ns in the t_nt.

T_d m_t K_n and Fr_d.

Complete the words

1. c_____r   3. p_____r   5. w_____d

2. g_____e   4. b_____f   6. d_____k

Write the answer next to the letter "A"

A: ___ **7.** They ___.

a. are bookshelves
b. is bookshelves
c. are bookshelfs

A: ___ **8.** What are these?

a. They are whiteboard.
b. They are whiteboards.
c. It is a whiteboard.

A: ___ **9.** Are these posters?

a. Yes, they is.
b. No, they are.
c. Yes, they are.

A: ___ **10.** Are those ___? Yes, they are.

a. books
b. blackboard
c. bookshelf

Answers on Page 156

Lesson 3

- Learn the words
- Learn the sentences
- Learn the phonics
- Test yourself!

Colors

кольори

Learn the words

1. **red**
червоний

2. **yellow**
жовтий

3. **green**
зелений

4. **blue**
синій

5. **purple**
фіолетовий

6. **orange**
помаранчевий

7. **brown**
коричневий

8. **pink**
рожевий

9. **black**
чорний

10. **white**
білий

Write the missing letters!

1. r_ _

2. y_ _l_w

3. g_e_n

4. b_u_

5. p_ _p_e

6. o_a_ _e

7. b_o_ _

8. p_ _ _

9. b_a_ _

10. w_i _ _

Have fun with the words!

Write the 3 missing words

1._____
2._____
3._____

green
red
blue
yellow
pink
black
orange

1._____
2._____
3._____

black
purple
yellow
white
brown
pink
blue

1._____
2._____
3._____

white
purple
orange
brown
red
black
green

1._____
2._____
3._____

orange
purple
white
green
pink
yellow
blue

1._____
2._____
3._____

purple
black
brown
green
orange
red
white

1._____
2._____
3._____

black
blue
brown
pink
yellow
red
green

What color is this?

It is <u>yellow</u>.

It isn't <u>green</u>.

What color is that?

It is <u>purple</u>.

It isn't <u>blue</u>.

Write the missing words!

What _____ is this?

It is _____ .

It _____ .

What _____ _____ that?

It _____ .

_____ isn't _____ .

_____ _____ _____ this?

_____ is _____ .

_____ _____ white.

_____ ?

_____ .

_____ .

Is this <u>pen</u> <u>red</u>?

Yes, it is.

No, it isn't. It is <u>brown</u>.

Is that <u>crayon</u> <u>pink</u>?

Yes, it is.

No, it isn't. It is <u>orange</u>.

Write the missing words!

Is this apple _____?

Yes, it _____.

No, it _____. It's _____.

Is _____ chair _____?

Yes, _____ is.

_____, it _____. It is _____.

_____ this _____ _____?

Yes, _____ _____.

No, _____ _____. It _____ _____.

_____?

_____.

_____.

_____.

i /ɪ/

big /bɪg/

pig /pɪg/

bin /bɪn/

6

six /sɪks/

More words

sit

dig

little

fix

kick

Write the words

i /ɪ/

Write the letters & Read the sentences!

Th_s p_g _s b_g.

I f_x s_x b_ns.

I s_t on the l_ttle bench w_th h_m.

Complete the words

1. y_____w   3. o_____e   5. b_____k

2. b_____n   4. g_____n   6. p_____e

Write the answer next to the letter "A"

A: ___ **7.** What color ___?

a. is these
b. is this
c. are that

A: ___ **8.** What color is that?

a. It is a green.
b. Its purple.
c. It is blue.

A: ___ **9.** Is this pen blue?

a. Yes, it is.
b. Yes it is.
c. No, it is. It's red.

A: ___ **10.** Is that ___?

a. brown desk
b. desk brown
c. desks brown

Answers on Page 156

Lesson

4

- Learn the words
- Learn the sentences
- Learn the phonics
- Test yourself!

My family

моя родина

Learn the words

1. **grandmother**
   бабуся

2. **grandfather**
   дідусь

3. **baby sister**
   молодша сестра

4. **baby brother**
   молодший брат

5. **aunt**
   тітка

6. **uncle**
   дядько

7. **sister**
   сестра

8. **brother**
   брат

9. **mother**
   мати

10. **father**
    батько

Write the missing letters!

1. g_a_ _m_t_e_

2. g_a_df_ _h_ _

3. b_ _y s_s_ _r

4. b_b_ b_o_h_ _

5. a_n_

6. _n_ _e

7. s_ _ _e_

8. b_o_h_ _

9. m_t_ _ _

10. f_ _h_ _

Have fun with the words!

Circle the family words!

1. pencil   (mother)   chair   purple   oval

2. heart   whiteboard   father   eraser   red

3. ruler   sister   poster   square   black

4. pink   computer   uncle   whiteout   chair

5. clock   glue   triangle   white   aunt

6. pen   blue   grandmother   star   globe

7. brother   marker   blackboard   circle   white

8. yellow   grandfather   desk   book   tape

Write the 8 words

1.	3.	5.	7.
2.	4.	6.	8.

Who is she?   Who is he?

She is my <u>mother</u>.   He is my <u>uncle</u>.

She isn't my <u>aunt</u>. He isn't my <u>father</u>.

Write the missing words!

Who _____ he?

He is my _____ .

He _____ my _____ .

Who _____ _____ ?

She is _____ _____ .

_____ isn't _____ _____ .

_____ _____ he?

_____ is _____ _____ .

He _____ my _____ .

_____ ?

_____ .

_____ .

Is she your <u>sister</u>?   Is he your <u>brother</u>?

Yes, she is.   Yes, he is.

No, she isn't.   No, he isn't.

Write the missing words!

Is he your _____ _____?

Yes, he _____.

No, he _____.

Is _____ your _____ sister?

Yes, _____ is.

_____, she _____.

_____ he _____ _____?

Yes, _____ _____.

No, _____ _____.

_____?

_____.

_____.

o /ɒ/

box /bɒks/

pot /pɒt/

frog /frɒg/

sock /sɒk/

More words

hot

from

got

Tom

stop

Write the words

o /ɒ/

Write the letters & Read the sentences!

The p_t is n_t h_t.

A s_ck is _n t_p _f the b_x.

T_m g_t a fr_g fr_m the sh_p.

Complete the words

1. b_____r   3. u_____e   5. f_____r

2. s_____r   4. a_____t   6. m_____r

Write the answer next to the letter "A"

A: ___ **7.** ___ is she?

a. What
b. Who
c. Whose

A: ___ **8.** ___ is my uncle.

a. She's
b. She
c. He

A: ___ **9.** Is she your sister?

a. Yes, it is.
b. Yes, she is.
c. No, she is.

A: ___ **10.** Is he ___?

a. your father
b. your aunt
c. you're brother

Answers on Page 156

Lesson
5
- Learn the words
- Learn the sentences
- Learn the phonics
- Test yourself!

Shapes

фігури

Learn the words

1. square квадрат	**6. star** зірка
2. circle коло	**7. rectangle** прямокутник
3. triangle трикутник	**8. octagon** восьмикутник
4. oval овал	**9. heart** серце
5. diamond ромб	**10. pentagon** п'ятикутник

Write the missing letters!

1. s_ _a_e

2. c_rcl_

3. tr_a_g_e

4. o_ _ _

5. d_a_o_ _

6. _t_ _

7. r_ _t_n_le

8. oc_a_o_

9. h_ _r_

10. p_n_ _ _o_

Have fun with the words!

Find the 8 shapes!

eraser whiteboard pentagon

oval crayon clock sister

apple uncle yellow

book triangle

green whiteout

chair square

pink grandfather

star heart

pencil desk

computer blue marker

diamond mother circle

brother bookshelf father

Write the 8 shapes

1.	3.	5.	7.
2.	4.	6.	8.

What is this shape?   What are these shapes?

It's a <u>square</u>.   They're <u>octagons</u>.

It isn't a <u>rectangle</u>.   They aren't <u>pentagons</u>.

Write the missing words!

What _____ this _____ ?

_____ a star.

It _____ a _____ .

What _____ these shapes?

_____ diamonds.

They aren't _____ .

What _____ this _____ ?

_____ a _____ .

_____ an _____ .

_____ ?

_____ .

_____ .

Is this a <u>triangle</u>?

Yes, it is.

No, it isn't.

Are these <u>star</u>s?

Yes, they are.

No, they aren't.

Write the missing words!

Is this an _____?

Yes, _____ is.

No, it _____ .

_____ these _____?

Yes, _____ are.

No, _____ _____ .

_____ this _____ _____?

_____ , _____ is.

No, _____ _____ .

_____?

_____.

_____.

U /ʌ/

hut /hʌt/

bus /bʌs/

mug /mʌg/

sun /sʌn/

More words

sum

fun

bun

jump

cut

Write the words

U /ʌ/

Write the letters & Read the sentences!

Have f_n in the s_n.

My m_g is on the b_s.

R_n and j_mp to the h_t.

Complete the words

1. s_____r   3. o_____n   5. h_____t

2. t_____e   4. r_____e   6. d_____d

Write the answer next to the letter "A"

A: ___ **7.** What ___ shape?

a. are these
b. is this
c. is it

A: ___ **8.** ___ aren't ___.

a. It, heart
b. They're, hearts
c. They, hearts

A: ___ **9.** Is this a pentagon?

a. Yes, it is.
b. No, they aren't.
c. Yes, they are.

A: ___ **10.** ___ these ___ circles?

a. Are, shape
b. Is, a
c. Are, x

Answers on Page 156

Lesson 6
- Learn the words
- Learn the sentences
- Learn the phonics
- Test yourself!

At the zoo

в зоопарку

Learn the words

1. **monkey**
мавпа

2. **lion**
лев

3. **tiger**
тигр

4. **bear**
ведмідь

5. **rhino**
носоріг

6. **penguin**
пінгвін

7. **giraffe**
жирафа

8. **elephant**
слон

9. **crocodile**
крокодил

10. **kangaroo**
кенгуру

Write the missing letters!

1. m_n_ _y

2. l_ _ _

3. _ig_ _

4. _ _ a_

5. r_ _ _o

6. pe_g _ _n

7. gi_a_f_

8. el_ _ h_n_

9. _ro_od_ _e

10. k_n_ _r_o

Have fun with the words!

Word Search

```
e d z q f d k o v o s d j v m d y y
l f z d s o x s u o m f f x l g l y
e m k a n g a r o o o y d x k i b h
p g a o p q t n i j n u c p l r o m
h t d w e v n p a r k g g z i a e n
a u b b h b i o l p e p j v o f r j
n r p e n g u i n b y r b m v f d r
t s g c r o c o d i l e h e z e p c
m o v f a z m n f d l e t i a c r m
u i y p p v m j n e r y n i n r i m
v f i p m t i g e r x z h e d o k d
t v s k u y p a r e f w e c p v x e
```

Words are hidden → ↓ and ↘ .

kangaroo

lion

giraffe

tiger

elephant

bear

penguin

crocodile

rhino

monkey

What is that animal?   What are those animals?

That animal is a <u>tiger</u>.   Those animals are <u>tiger</u>s.

That animal isn't a <u>rhino</u>.   Those animals aren't <u>lion</u>s.

Write the missing words!

What _____ that _____ ?

_____ animal is a _____ .

That animal _____ a _____ .

_____ are _____ animals?

Those _____ _____ rhinos.

They aren't _____ .

What _____ animal?

That _____ an _____ .

_____ animal _____ a _____ .

_____ ?

_____ .

_____ .

Is that animal a <u>giraffe</u>?   Are those <u>bear</u>s?

Yes, that's a giraffe.   Yes, those are bears.

No, that isn't a giraffe.   No, those aren't bears.

Write the missing words!

Is _____ animal a _____ ?

Yes, _____ a penguin.

No, that _____ a _____ .

_____ those tigers?

Yes, those _____ _____ .

No, _____ _____ tigers.

_____ that _____ _____ ?

_____ , _____ rhino.

_____ , that _____ a _____ .

_____ ?

_____ .

_____ .

OU /aʊ/

mouth /maʊθ/

loud /laʊd/

cloud /klaʊd/

round /raʊnd/

More words

out

about

sound

shout

found

Write the words

OU /aʊ/

Write the letters & Read the sentences!

I f_ _nd a r_ _nd circle.

That is a big cl_ _d.

The lion has a l_ _d m_ _th.

Complete the words

1. s ____ e   3. p ____ k   5. s ____ t

2. c ____ a   4. r ____ t   6. g ____ m

Write the answer next to the letter "A"

A: ___ **7.** What ___ animals?

a. are those
b. is that
c. is this

A: ___ **8.** That ___ is a ___.

a. animals, kangaroo
b. animal, bears
c. animal, crocodile

A: ___ **9.** Are those monkeys?

a. Yes, those are monkey.
b. No, those aren't monkeys.
c. Yes, that's a monkey.

A: ___ **10.** ___ that animal a ___?

a. Are, rhinos
b. Is, rhino
c. Are, rhino

Answers on Page 156

Lesson 7

- Learn the words
- Learn the sentences
- Learn the phonics
- Test yourself!

Jobs

професії

Learn the words

1. **doctor**
лікар

2. **chef**
повар

3. **nurse**
медсестра

4. **police officer**
поліцейський

5. **taxi driver**
таксист

6. **teacher**
вчитель

7. **farmer**
фермер

8. **salesclerk**
продавець

9. **firefighter**
пожежник

10. **builder**
будівельник

Write the missing letters!

1. d_ _to_

2. c_e_

3. n_rs_

4. p_ _i_e of_ic_ _

5. _a_i d_i_e_

6. te_c_ _r

7. fa_ _ _r

8. s_ _e_c_e_ _

9. f_r_ _i_h_er

10. b_i_d_ _

Have fun with the words!

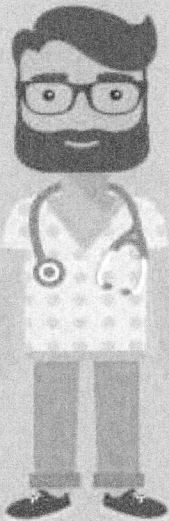

f i r e f i g h t e r

salesclerk
farmer
police officer
doctor
teacher

chef
builder
nurse
firefighter
taxi driver

What's his job?

He's a <u>nurse</u>.

He's not a <u>builder</u>.

What's her job?

She's a <u>doctor</u>.

She's not a <u>chef</u>.

Write the missing words!

What's _____ _____?

He's a _____.

_____ a salesclerk.

_____ her _____?

_____ a _____.

She's not _____ _____.

_____ his _____?

He's a _____ driver.

_____ a _____.

_____ ?

_____ .

_____ .

Is he a <u>police officer</u>?   Is she a <u>salesclerk</u>?

Yes, he is.   Yes, she is.

No, he's a <u>firefighter</u>.   No, she's a <u>teacher</u>.

Write the missing words!

Is _____ a _____ officer?

Yes, he _____.

No, _____ a _____.

_____ she a _____?

Yes, _____ _____.

No, she's _____ taxi _____.

_____ he _____ _____?

_____, _____ _____.

_____, _____ a _____.

_____?

_____.

_____.

OW /aʊ/

COW /kaʊ/

towel /ˈtaʊəl/

down /daʊn/

shower /ˈʃaʊər/

More words

now

crowd

town

allow

how

Write the words

OW /aʊ/

Write the letters & Read the sentences!

H_ _ is that c_ _ out?

W_ _! There is a big cr_ _d d_ _nt_ _n.

Take a sh_ _er n_ _.

Complete the words

1. b_____r

3. s_____k

5. t_____r

2. n_____e

4. d_____r

6. c_____f

Write the answer next to the letter "A"

A: ___ **7.** ___ his job?

a. Who's
b. What's
c. What

A: ___ **8.** She's ___ a firefighter.

a. isn't
b. is
c. not

A: ___ **9.** Is he a teacher?

a. No, she's a salesclerk.
b. No, he's a nurse.
c. No, he a doctor.

A: ___ **10.** Is she ___?

a. a farmer
b. an nurse
c. police officer

Answers on Page 156

Lesson 8

- Learn the words
- Learn the sentences
- Learn the phonics
- Test yourself!

At the fruit market

на фруктовому ринку

Learn the words

1. **apple**
   яблуко

2. **orange**
   апельсин

3. **lemon**
   лимон

4. **banana**
   банан

5. **watermelon**
   кавун

6. **pineapple**
   ананас

7. **strawberry**
   полуниця

8. **grape**
   виноград

9. **cherry**
   вишня

10. **pear**
    груша

Write the missing letters!

1. _p_l_

2. o_ _ _g_

3. l_m_ _

4. ba_ _n_

5. w_t_ _m_ _o_

6. p_n_a_ _l

7. s_ _a_ _er_ _

8. g_a_e

9. c_e_ _y

10. p_ _ _

Have fun with the words!

Write the 3 missing words

1._____

2. _____

3. _____

> apple
>
> lemon
>
> banana
>
> cherry
>
> strawberry
>
> watermelon
>
> pear

1._____

2. _____

3. _____

> cherry
>
> pineapple
>
> apple
>
> watermelon
>
> orange
>
> lemon
>
> grape

1._____

2. _____

3. _____

> pineapple
>
> strawberry
>
> orange
>
> banana
>
> grape
>
> pear
>
> cherry

1._____

2. _____

3. _____

> pear
>
> lemon
>
> grape
>
> apple
>
> watermelon
>
> banana
>
> pineapple

1._____

2. _____

3. _____

> pineapple
>
> strawberry
>
> orange
>
> cherry
>
> watermelon
>
> grape
>
> lemon

1._____

2. _____

3. _____

> strawberry
>
> apple
>
> pineapple
>
> banana
>
> lemon
>
> pear
>
> orange

Which fruit do you want?   Which fruit does he want?

I want a <u>strawberry</u>.   He wants an <u>apple</u>.

I don't want a <u>lemon</u>.   He doesn't want a <u>banana</u>.

Write the missing words!

Which _____ do you _____?

I want a _____.

I _____ want a _____.

_____ fruit _____ she want?

She _____ a _____.

She _____ want an _____.

_____ fruit _____ you _____?

I _____ _____ _____.

_____ don't _____ a _____.

_____?

_____.

_____.

Do you want a <u>grape</u>?

Yes, I do.

No, I don't.

Does she want an <u>orange</u>?

Yes, she does.

No, she doesn't.

Write the missing words!

Do _____ want a _____?

Yes, I _____.

No, _____ _____.

_____ he _____ a _____?

_____, _____ does.

No, he _____.

_____ you _____ an _____?

Yes, _____ _____.

_____, I _____.

_____?

_____.

_____.

OW /ou/

snow /snou/

bowl /boul/

bow /bou/

arrow /'ærou/

More words

grow

slow

mow

blow

crow

Write the words

OW /ou/

Write the letters & Read the sentences!

Your yell_ _ b_ _ is in the b_ _l.

The grass gr_ _s sl_ _ly.

The black cr_ _ is in the sn_ _.

Complete the words

1. s_____y   3. w_____n   5. b_____a

2. c_____y   4. p_____e   6. l_____n

Write the answer next to the letter "A"

A: ___ **7.** Which fruit ___ she ___?

a. do, want
b. does, want
c. does, wants

A: ___ **8.** I ___ pineapple.

a. want a
b. wants a
c. want an

A: ___ **9.** Do you want a watermelon?

a. Yes, I does.
b. No, I do.
c. No, I don't.

A: ___ **10.** Does ___ want ___ orange?

a. he, a
b. you, an
c. she, an

Answers on Page 156

Lesson 9

- Learn the words
- Learn the sentences
- Learn the phonics
- Test yourself!

The body

тіло

Learn the words

1. **arm**
рука

2. **stomach**
живіт

3. **shoulder**
плече

4. **head**
голова

5. **neck**
шия

6. **toe**
палець на нозі

7. **foot**
ступня

8. **finger**
палець

9. **hand**
кисть руки

10. **leg**
нога

Write the missing letters!

1. _ _m

2. s_o_ _c_

3. _h_ _ld_r

4. _e_ _

5. n_ _ _

6. t_ _

7. _ _ _t

8. f_n_e_

9. h_ _ _

10. l_ _

Have fun with the words!

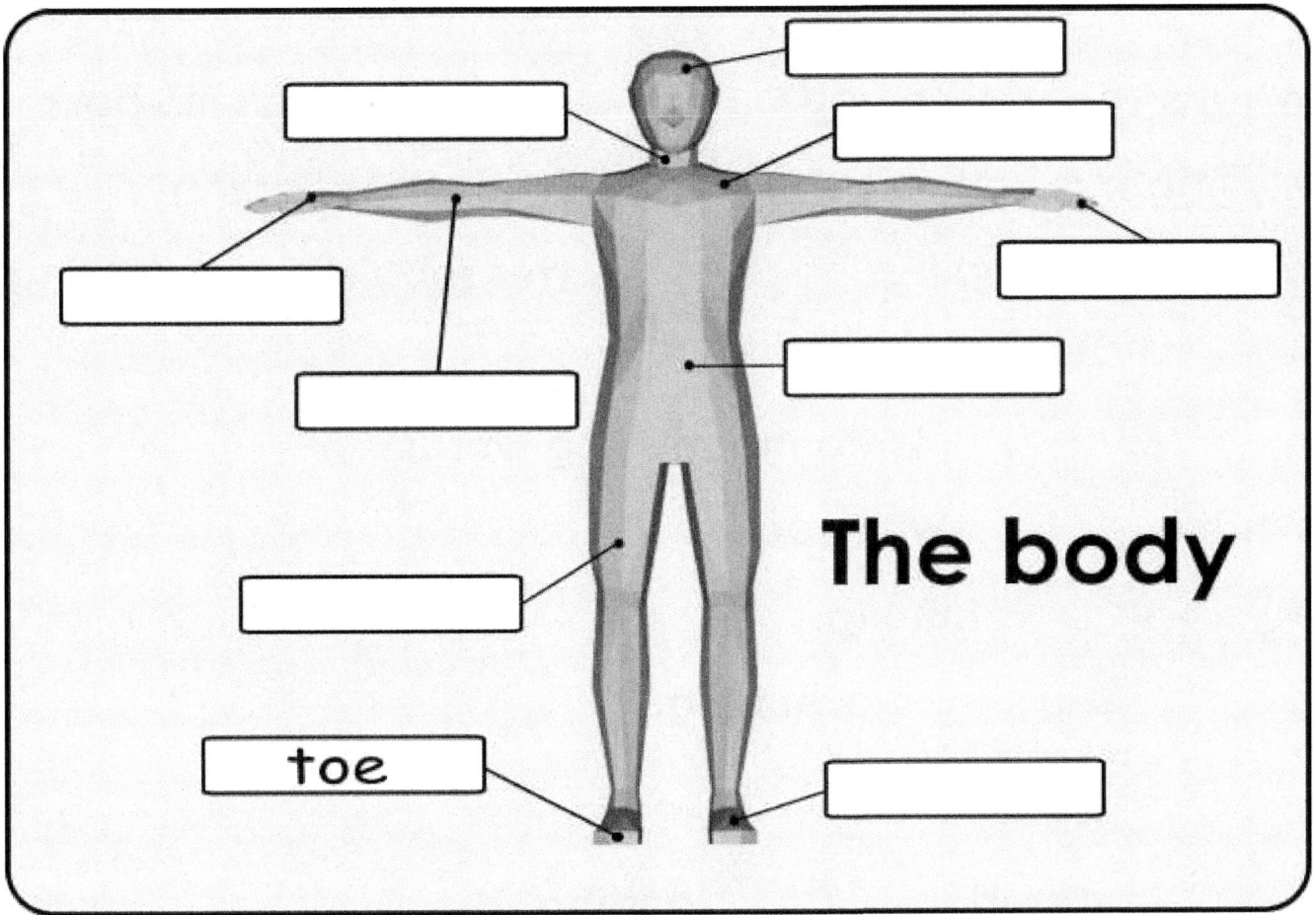

The body

toe

Unscramble the letters!

1. helosurd _____

2. nfgire _____

3. atohmcs _____

4. enkc _____

5. nhda _____

What's wrong with <u>you</u>?

My <u>finger</u> is hurting.

My <u>toe</u> isn't hurting.

What's wrong with <u>her</u>?

Her <u>arm</u> is hurting.

Her <u>shoulder</u> isn't hurting.

Write the missing words!

What's _____ with you?

My _____ is hurting.

_____ leg _____ hurting.

_____ wrong _____ her?

_____ stomach _____ hurting.

Her _____ isn't _____.

What's _____ _____ him?

His _____ .

_____ toe _____ _____ .

_____ ?

_____ .

_____ .

Is your <u>neck</u> hurting?   Is his <u>leg</u> hurting?

Yes, my neck is hurting.   Yes, her leg is hurting.

No, my neck isn't hurting.   No, her leg isn't hurting.

Write the missing words!

Is _____ arm _____ ?

Yes, _____ arm _____ hurting.

No, my _____ isn't _____ .

_____ his _____ _____ ?

_____ , his _____ is _____ .

No, _____ hand _____ _____ .

_____ her _____ _____ ?

Yes, _____ foot _____ _____ .

_____ , her _____ _____ .

_____ ?

_____ .

_____ .

oa /ou/

coat /kout/

boat /bout/

soap /soup/

loaf /louf/

More words

goal

road

float

oats

toad

Write the words

oa /ou/

Write the letters & Read the sentences!

A t_ _d is on the r_ _d.

The s_ _p is on my c_ _t.

That b_ _t doesn't fl_ _t.

Complete the words

1. s_____h   3. f_____t   5. s_____r

2. h_____d   4. f_____r   6. n_____k

Write the answer next to the letter "A"

A: ___ **7.** What's wrong with you?

a. His toe is hurting.
b. Her toe is hurting.
c. My toe is hurting.

A: ___ **8.** His shoulder ___.

a. are hurting
b. is hurting
c. is hurt

A: ___ **9.** Is her neck hurting?

a. Yes, his neck is hurting.
b. No, her neck isn't hurting.
c. Yes, her nose is hurting.

A: ___ **10.** Is ___ leg hurting? Yes, my leg is leg hurting.

a. your
b. his
c. her

Answers on Page 156

Lesson

10

- Learn the words
- Learn the sentences
- Learn the phonics
- Test yourself!

Sports

спорт

Learn the words

1. **basketball**
баскетбол

2. **badminton**
бадмінтон

3. **golf**
гольф

4. **hockey**
хокей

5. **soccer**
футбол

6. **cricket**
крикет

7. **baseball**
бейсбол

8. **volleyball**
волейбол

9. **football**
футбол

10. **tennis**
теніс

Write the missing letters!

1. b_s_e_b_ _l

2. b_d_ _n_o_

3. g_ _ _ _

4. h_c_e_

5. _o_ce_

6. c_i_k_t

7. _ _s_b_l_

8. v_l_e_b_ _l

9. _o_t_ _l

10. t_n_ _s

Have fun with the words!

soccer •

basketball •

golf •

tennis •

hockey •

Unscramble the letters!

1. bbsaalel

_____

2. lolvleaybl

_____

3. lfotbalo

_____

4. rctkice

_____

5. nbdmtinao

_____

Which sports do you like?   Which sports does he like?

I like <u>baseball</u> and <u>golf</u>.   He likes <u>tennis</u> and <u>hockey</u>.

I don't like <u>cricket</u>.   He doesn't like <u>volleyball</u>.

Write the missing words!

Which _____ do you like?

I _____ baseball and _____.

I _____ like _____.

_____ sports _____ he like?

He _____ _____ and cricket.

He _____ _____ _____.

Which _____ does _____ _____?

_____ likes football _____ _____.

She _____ _____.

_____ _____?

_____.

_____.

Do you like <u>badminton</u>?

Does she like <u>tennis</u>?

Yes, I do.

Yes, she does.

No, I don't.

No, she doesn't.

Write the missing words!

Do you _____ _____?

Yes, _____ _____.

No, _____ _____.

_____ he _____ _____?

_____, he _____.

No, _____ _____.

_____ she _____ _____?

Yes, _____ _____.

_____, _____ doesn't.

_____?

_____.

_____.

ee /i/

sheep /ʃip/

street /strit/

bee /bi/

jeep /dʒip/

More words

see

keep

knee

teeth

deep

Write the words

ee /i/

Write the letters & Read the sentences!

I s_ _ a j_ _p on the str_ _t.

A b_ _ is on the sh_ _p's kn_ _.

She k_ _ps her t_ _th clean.

Complete the words

1. t_____s   3. g_____f   5. b_____n

2. v_____l   4. c_____t   6. h_____y

Write the answer next to the letter "A"

A: ___ **7.** Which sports ___ you like?

a. do
b. does
c. is

A: ___ **8.** He ___ volleyball.

a. don't like
b. doesn't likes
c. doesn't like

A: ___ **9.** Does she like badminton?

a. Yes, she does.
b. No, he doesn't.
c. No, she does.

A: ___ **10.** ___ you like tennis?

a. Does
b. Do
c. Are

Answers on Page 156

Lesson 11
- Learn the words
- Learn the sentences
- Learn the phonics
- Test yourself!

Places

місця

Learn the words

1. **store**
магазин

2. **swimming pool**
басейн

3. **department store**
універмаг

4. **supermarket**
супермаркет

5. **night market**
нічний ринок

6. **cinema**
кінотеатр

7. **beach**
пляж

8. **park**
парк

9. **gym**
спортзал

10. **restaurant**
ресторан

Write the missing letters!

1. s _ o _ _

2. sw _ m _ i g p _ _l

3. d _ p _ _ t _ e _ t s _ o _ e

4. su _ _ r _ a _ k _ _

5. n _ _ _ t m _ r _ e _

6. c _ n _ _ _

7. b _ a _ _

8. p _ _ _

9. g _ _

10. r _ s _ a _ r _ _ t

Have fun with the words!

Word Search

```
k u w t n v a h l g d r w t y n n a
w u w d c s w i m m i n g p o o l g
n i g h t m a r k e t m r b k y z z
l s u p e r m a r k e t y p l r t m
l l n l i x o d w r u d y y a m n s
u g s b a o z b x a w c p a z r x h
a u f e d y q k m h l p z g y m k m
d e p a r t m e n t s t o r e t q d
s n t c z y c i n e m a g r a c p q
c z f h p o s t o r e v d n s i z i
v u p l u r o t y u c y e p w r b o
v v b a r e s t a u r a n t b e c c
```

Word directions: → ➘ ↓

beach

cinema

department store

gym

night market

park

restaurant

store

supermarket

swimming pool

Where do you want to go?   Where does he want to go?

I want to go to the <u>beach</u>.   He wants to go to the <u>store</u>.

I don't want to go to the <u>gym</u>.   He doesn't want to go to the <u>gym</u>.

Write the missing words!

Where _____ you want _____ go?

I want to _____ to the _____ .

I _____ want to go _____ the department _____ .

_____ does _____ want to _____ ?

He _____ to go _____ the _____ pool.

He _____ want _____ go to the _____ .

Where _____ you _____ to _____ ?

I _____ to _____ _____ the _____ .

I _____ _____ to _____ to the _____ .

_____ ?

_____ .

_____ .

Do you want to go to the <u>park</u>?   Does she want to go to the <u>cinema</u>?

Yes, I do.   Yes, she does.

No, I don't want to.   No, she doesn't want to.

Write the missing words!

Do you _____ to _____ to the _____ pool?

Yes, _____ _____ .

No, I _____ _____ to.

_____ he _____ to go _____ the _____ ?

_____ , he _____ .

No, he _____ want _____ .

_____ you _____ to go to _____ _____ ?

Yes, _____ _____ .

_____ , I _____ _____ .

_____ ?

_____ .

_____ .

ea /i/

beach /biʧ/

read /rid/

leaf /lif/

bean /bin/

More words

jeans

cheap

team

wheat

clean

Write the words

ea /i/

Write the letters & Read the sentences!

These j_ _ns are r_ _lly ch_ _p.

A b_ _n is on the green l_ _f.

Pl_ _se cl_ _n the b_ _ch.

Complete the words

1. s_____e   3. p_____k   5. s_____t

2. c_____a   4. r_____t   6. g_____m

Write the answer next to the letter "A"

A: ___ **7.** Where ___ he want to go?

a. do
b. does
c. is

A: ___ **8.** I ___ go to the night market.

a. want
b. want to
c. wants to

A: ___ **9.** Does she want to go to the park?

a. No, she don't want to.
b. No, she does.
c. No, she doesn't want to.

A: ___ **10.** Do you want to ___ the swimming pool?

a. go to
b. go
c. goes to

Answers on Page 156

Lesson 12

- Learn the words
- Learn the sentences
- Learn the phonics
- Test yourself!

Clothes

одяг

Learn the words

1. **T-shirt**
   футболка

2. **blouse**
   блузка

3. **dress**
   плаття

4. **coat**
   пальто

5. **scarf**
   шарф

6. **hat**
   капелюх

7. **sweater**
   светр

8. **necktie**
   краватка

9. **skirt**
   спідниця

10. **jacket**
    куртка

Write the missing letters!

1. T-_ _ir_

2. b_o_s_

3. d_e_s_

4. c_ _t

5. s_ar_

6. h_ _

7. s_ea_e_

8. _e_kt_e

9. s_i_t

10. ja_k_t

Have fun with the words!

T-shirt
blouse
dress
coat
scarf

n e c k t i e

hat
sweater
necktie
skirt
jacket

What will you wear later?   What will he wear later?

I will wear a <u>dress</u>.   He will wear a <u>sweater</u>.

I won't wear a <u>skirt</u>.   He won't wear a <u>jacket</u>.

Write the missing words!

What _____ you _____ later?

I will _____ a _____ .

I _____ wear a _____ .

_____ will _____ wear _____ ?

He _____ wear _____ _____ .

He _____ _____ a _____ .

What _____ you _____ _____ ?

_____ will _____ a skirt.

I _____ _____ a _____ .

_____ ?

_____ .

_____ .

Will you wear a <u>necktie</u> later?

Yes, I will.

No, I won't.

Will she wear a <u>T-shirt</u> later?

Yes, she will.

No, she won't.

Write the missing words!

Will you _____ a _____ later?

Yes, I _____ .

No, _____ .

_____ he _____ a _____ _____ ?

_____ , he _____ .

No, _____ _____ .

_____ you _____ _____ _____ _____ ?

_____ , _____ will.

_____ , _____ _____ .

_____ ?

_____ .

_____ .

OO /u/

spoon /spun/

food /fud/

moon /mun/

pool /pul/

More words

tool

broom

boot

room

roof

Write the words

OO /u/

Write the letters & Read the sentences!

Eat your f_ _d with a sp_ _n.

There's a p_ _l in that r_ _m.

Use these t_ _ls to fix the r_ _f.

Complete the words

1. b____e   3. n____e   5. s____f

2. s____r   4. j____t   6. d____s

Write the answer next to the letter "A"

A: ___ **7.** What ___ he wear later?

a. do
b. will
c. does

A: ___ **8.** He ___ a coat.

a. won't wears
b. won't wear
c. will wears

A: ___ **9.** Will she wear a skirt later?

a. No, she won't.
b. No, she willn't.
c. No, she will.

A: ___ **10.** Will you wear ___ later?

a. a necktie
b. dress
c. hats

Answers on Page 156

Lesson
13
- Learn the words
- Learn the sentences
- Learn the phonics
- Test yourself!

School subjects

шкільні предмети

Learn the words

1. **English**
англійська

2. **computer**
інформатика

3. **social studies**
соціологія

4. **geography**
географія

5. **physical education (P.E.)**
фізична культура

6. **art**
образотворче мистецтво

7. **math**
математика

8. **science**
природничі науки

9. **history**
історія

10. **music**
музика

Write the missing letters!

1. E_g_i_h

2. c_m_ut_r

3. so_ _a_ s_ud_e_

4. g_o_r_p_y

5. p_y_i_al e_u_a_ _on

6. a_ _

7. m_ _ _

8. s_i_ _ce

9. hi_t_ _ _

10. _us_c

Have fun with the words!

Write the 3 missing words

1._____

2. _____

3. _____

> math
>
> English
>
> science
>
> physical education
>
> history
>
> social studies
>
> computer

1._____

2. _____

3. _____

> history
>
> music
>
> physical education
>
> art
>
> math
>
> geography
>
> science

1._____

2. _____

3. _____

> English
>
> math
>
> social studies
>
> geography
>
> computer
>
> art
>
> music

1._____

2. _____

3. _____

> math
>
> art
>
> physical education
>
> music
>
> science
>
> geography
>
> social studies

1._____

2. _____

3. _____

> history
>
> social studies
>
> music
>
> art
>
> English
>
> computer
>
> math

1._____

2. _____

3. _____

> science
>
> history
>
> physical education
>
> art
>
> computer
>
> English
>
> geography

What class do you have today?   What class does he have today?

Today, I have <u>geography</u> class.   Today, he has <u>English</u> class.

I don't have <u>music</u> class.   He doesn't have <u>math</u> class.

Write the missing words!

What _____ do you _____ today?

_____ , I have _____ class.

I _____ have _____ education _____ .

_____ class _____ she have _____ ?

Today, she _____ _____ class.

_____ _____ have _____ studies class.

What class _____ you _____ _____ ?

Today, _____ have _____ .

I _____ _____ math _____ .

_____ ?

_____ .

_____ .

Do you have <u>history</u> class today?   Does she have <u>art</u> class today?

Yes, I do.   Yes, she does.

No, I don't.   No, she doesn't.

Write the missing words!

Do you _____ social _____ class _____?

Yes, I _____ .

No, _____ .

_____ he _____ _____ class _____?

_____ , he _____ .

No, _____ _____ .

_____ you _____ physical _____ _____ today?

_____ , _____ do.

_____ , I _____ .

_____ ?

_____ .

_____ .

ai /eɪ/

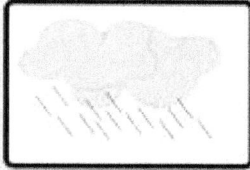

rain /reɪn/

chain /tʃeɪn/

mail /meɪl/

train /keɪv/

More words

aim

wait

pain

rail

tail

Write the words

ai /eɪ/

Write the letters & Read the sentences!

The sn_ _l is in the r_ _n ag_ _n.

I w_ _t for the tr_ _n.

There is b_ _t by the s_ _l.

Complete the words

1. g_____y   3. h_____y   5. E_____h

2. c_____r   4. m_____c   6. s_____e

Write the answer next to the letter "A"

A: ___ **7.** What class ___ today?

a. does she have
b. does you have
c. does he has

A: ___ **8.** Today, he ___ social studies class.

a. have
b. has
c. haves

A: ___ **9.** Do you have physical education class today?

a. Yes, I have.
b. Yes, I do.
c. Yes, I does.

A: ___ **10.** ___ she ___ math class today?

a. Does, has
b. Do, have
c. Does, have

Answers on Page 156

Lesson
14
- Learn the words
- Learn the sentences
- Learn the phonics
- Test yourself!

Vegetables

овочі

Learn the words

1. **potato**
картопля

2. **carrot**
морква

3. **pumpkin**
гарбуз

4. **broccoli**
брокколі

5. **asparagus**
спаржа

6. **cabbage**
капуста

7. **spinach**
шпинат

8. **corn**
кукурудза

9. **onion**
цибуля

10. **mushroom**
гриб

Write the missing letters!

1. p_t_t_

2. c_ _r_ _

3. _u_p_ _n

4. b_o_ _ol_

5. _s_a_ _g_s

6. c_b_a_e

7. s_i_a_ _

8. _o_ _

9. _n_o_

10. m_s_ _o_ _

Have fun with the words!

Circle the vegetable words!

1. golf   (carrot)   art   park   stomach

2. beach   asparagus   neck   eraser   lemon

3. history   tennis   pumpkin   leg   gym

4. grape   computer   onion   hockey   music

5. spinach   hat   apple   store   foot

6. pen   head   badminton   skirt   corn

7. blouse   potato   arm   circle   pear

8. orange   jacket   desk   cabbage   finger

Write the 8 words

| 1. | 3. | 5. | 7. |
| 2. | 4. | 6. | 8. |

What did you eat for dinner?   What did they eat for dinner?

We ate <u>corn</u> for dinner.   They ate <u>broccoli</u> for dinner.

We didn't eat <u>mushroom</u>.   They didn't eat <u>asparagus</u>.

Write the missing words!

What _____ you _____ for dinner?

We _____ spinach for _____ .

We _____ eat _____ .

What _____ they _____ for _____ ?

They _____ _____ for _____ .

_____ didn't _____ _____ .

What _____ you _____ _____ _____ ?

I _____ _____ .

_____ _____ eat _____ for _____ .

_____ ?

_____ .

_____ .

Did you eat <u>broccoli</u> for dinner?   Did they eat <u>potato</u> for dinner?

Yes, we did.   Yes, they did.

No, we didn't. We ate <u>cabbage</u>.   No, they didn't. They ate <u>onion</u>.

Write the missing words!

Did you _____ asparagus _____ dinner?

Yes, we _____ .

No, _____ didn't. We _____ .

_____ they eat _____ for _____ ?

_____ , they _____ .

No, _____ _____ . They ate _____ .

Did you _____ _____ dinner?

Yes, _____ _____ .

_____ , we _____ . We _____ _____ .

_____ ?

_____ .

_____ .

a_e /eɪ/

cake /keɪk/

wave /'weɪv/

name /neɪm/

cave /keɪv/

More words

shape

lake

make

take

late

Write the words

a_e /eɪ/

Write the letters & Read the sentences!

His n_m_ is the s_m_ as mine.

There is a c_v_ near the l_k_.

You can t_k_ the c_k_ home.

Complete the words

1. c_____t   3. b_____i   5. m_____m

2. p_____o   4. s_____h   6. o_____n

Write the answer next to the letter "A"

A: ___ **7.** What did you eat ___ dinner?

a. of
b. for
c. on

A: ___ **8.** They ___ pumpkin.

a. didn't ate
b. didn't eaten
c. didn't eat

A: ___ **9.** Did you eat spinach for dinner?

a. No, we didn't. We ate potato.
b. No, we didn't. We eat cabbage.
c. No, we did. We ate corn.

A: ___ **10.** Did they ___ mushroom for dinner?

a. ate
b. eats
c. eat

Answers on Page 156

Lesson
15
- Learn the words
- Learn the sentences
- Learn the phonics
- Test yourself!

At the toy shop

у магазині іграшок

Learn the words

1. **car**
машинка

2. **airplane**
Літак

3. **dinosaur**
динозавр

4. **doll**
лялька

5. **teddy bear**
плюшевий ведмедик

6. **jump rope**
скакалка

7. **board game**
настільна гра

8. **toy block**
конструктор

9. **robot**
робот

10. **ball**
м'яч

Write the missing letters!

1. c_ _

2. a_r_la_e

3. d_n_sa_r

4. do_ _

5. t_d_y b_a_

6. ju_p r_p_

7. b_a_d ga_e

8. t_y b_oc_s

9. r_bo_

10. _al_

Have fun with the words!

car•

toy block•

jump rope•

dinosaur•

teddy bear•

Unscramble the letters!

1. analirpe _____

2. oldl _____

3. robad agem _____

4. albl _____

5. broto _____

What are you playing with?   What is she playing with?

I am playing with my <u>dinosaur</u>.   She is playing with her <u>robot</u>.

I'm not playing with my <u>jump rope</u>.   She's not playing with her <u>doll</u>.

Write the missing words!

What _____ you _____ with?

I _____ playing _____ my _____.

I'm _____ with _____ board _____.

What _____ he _____?

He _____ with _____.

_____ not _____ his _____.

_____ is _____ playing _____?

She _____ with _____ jump _____.

_____ playing _____ her _____.

_____?

_____.

_____.

Are you playing with your <u>car</u>?   Is he playing with his <u>ball</u>?

Yes, I am.   Yes, he is.

No, I'm playing with my <u>doll</u>.   No, he's playing with his <u>robot</u>.

Write the missing words!

Are you _____ with _____ _____?

Yes, I _____.

No, _____ playing _____ my _____.

_____ she _____ her _____ blocks?

_____, _____ is.

No, _____ _____ with _____ _____ bear.

Is _____ _____ with _____ _____?

_____, he _____.

_____, _____ _____ his _____.

_____?

_____.

_____.

i_e /aɪ/

bike /baɪk/

time /taɪm/

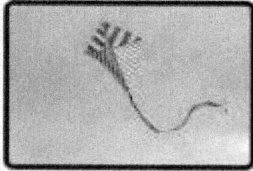

kite /kaɪt/

dice /daɪs/

More words

white

bite

size

mine

like

Write the words

i_e /aɪ/

Write the letters & Read the sentences!

The wh_t_ b_k_ is m_n_.

I l_k_ this k_t_.

The small s_z_ is f_n_.

Complete the words

1. a_____e   3. r_____t   5. b_____l

2. d_____r   4. t_____r 6. d_____l

Write the answer next to the letter "A"

A: ___ **7.** What ___ she playing ___?

a. are, with
b. is, of
c. is, with

A: ___ **8.** He is ___ teddy bear.

a. play with his
b. playing with his
c. playing with her

A: ___ **9.** Are you playing with your jump rope?

a. No, I'm playing with my dinosaur.
b. No, I playing with my toy blocks.
c. Yes, I are.

A: ___ **10.** ___ playing with ___ doll?

a. Is you, your
b. Is she, her
c. Are she, her

Answers on Page 156

Lesson
16
- Learn the words
- Learn the sentences
- Learn the phonics
- Test yourself!

In the kitchen

на кухні а

Learn the words

1. **refrigerator**
холодильник

2. **cupboard**
шафа

3. **microwave oven**
мікрохвильова піч

4. **dish rack**
стійка для посуду

5. **coffee maker**
кавоварка

6. **toaster**
тостер

7. **stove**
піч

8. **pan**
tava

9. **rice cooker**
рисоварка

10. **blender**
блендер

Write the missing letters!

1. _ef_i_era_or

2. c_p_o_ _d

3. m_c_ow_ _e o_ _n

4. d_s_ ra_ _

5. _o_f_e m_k_ _

6. to_s_e_

7. _to_ _

8. p_ _

9. r_c_ c_ok_ _

10. _l_nd_r

- 96 -

Have fun with the words!

Find the 8 kitchen items!

banana   hockey   crocodile

doctor   foot   teacher

ball   refrigerator   tennis

yellow   pan   robot

lion   head   elephant

giraffe   math   blender   Pencil

baseball

monkey   arm   eraser

cupboard   computer   stove

square   star   rice cooker

circle

dish rack   toaster   father

Write the 8 shapes

| 1. | 3. | 5. | 7. |
| 2. | 4. | 6. | 8. |

What does your kitchen need?

Our kitchen needs a new <u>stove</u>.

It doesn't need a <u>rice cooker</u>.

Write the missing words!

What _____ your _____ need?

_____ kitchen _____ a _____ _____ .

It _____ a _____ rack.

What _____ _____ kitchen _____ ?

Their _____ needs _____ _____ .

_____ doesn't _____ a microwave _____ .

_____ does _____ _____ ?

Our _____ _____ new _____ .

_____ need _____ _____ .

_____ ?

_____ .

_____ .

Does their kitchen need a new <u>refrigerator</u>?

Yes, their kitchen does.

No, it doesn't need a new one.

Write the missing words!

Does _____ kitchen _____ a new _____?

_____, our _____ does.

No, _____ _____ need a _____ _____.

Does their _____ need a _____ _____ maker?

Yes, _____ kitchen _____.

_____, it doesn't _____ _____ _____ one.

_____ your _____ a _____ _____?

_____, _____ _____ does.

No, _____ _____ new _____.

_____?

_____.

_____.

o_e /oʊ/

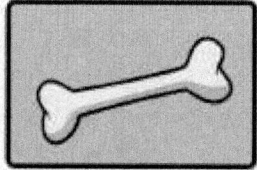

bone /boʊn/

rope /roʊp/

cone /koʊn/

rose /roʊz/

More words

nose

alone

stone

woke

globe

Write the words

o_e /oʊ/

Write the letters & Read the sentences!

A r_s_ is on the st_n_.

The dog smells the b_n_ with its n_s_.

He r_d_ his bike al_n_.

Complete the words

1. b____r   3. p____n   5. c____d

2. s____e   4. t____r   6. r____r

Write the answer next to the letter "A"

A: ___ **7.** What ___ your kitchen ___?

a. does, need
b. does, needs
c. do, need

A: ___ **8.** It ___ need a microwave oven.

a. does'nt
b. doesn't
c. don't

A: ___ **9.** Does your kitchen need a new dish rack?

a. Yes, our kitchen does.
b. No, it does need a new one.
c. Yes, their kitchen does.

A: ___ **10.** ___ kitchen need a new stove?

a. Does they're
b. Does there
c. Does their

Answers on Page 156

Lesson 17
- Learn the words
- Learn the sentences
- Learn the phonics
- Test yourself!

Feelings

почуття

Learn the words

1. **fine**
в порядку

2. **sad**
сумний

3. **bored**
знуджений

4. **energetic**
енергійний

5. **tired**
втомлений

6. **angry**
сердитий

7. **happy**
щасливий

8. **excited**
збуджений

9. **frustrated**
розчарований

10. **sick**
хворий

Write the missing letters!

1. _in_

2. _a_

3. _o_ _d

4. e_er_et_ _

5. t_r_ _

6. a_g_ _

7. _a_ _y

8. _xci_e_

9. f_u_t_a_ _d

10. s_c_

Have fun with the words!

happy

angry

sick

tired

sad

Unscramble the letters!

1. nregetiec

2. rdufsrtaet

3. dbreo

4. xectdei

5. inef

How are you feeling now?   How is he feeling now?

I'm feeling <u>energetic</u>.   He's feeling <u>fine</u>.

I'm not feeling <u>tired</u>.   He isn't feeling <u>angry</u>.

Write the missing words!

How _____ you _____ now?

_____ feeling _____ .

I'm _____ energetic.

How _____ he _____ _____ ?

He's _____ happy.

_____ feeling _____ .

_____ are _____ feeling _____ ?

I'm _____ .

_____ frustrated.

_____ ?

_____ .

_____ .

Are you feeling <u>frustrated</u> now?   Is she feeling <u>bored</u> now?

Yes, I am.   Yes, she is.

No, I'm feeling <u>happy</u>.   No, she's feeling <u>excited</u>.

Write the missing words!

Are _____ feeling _____ now?

Yes, I _____.

No, _____ feeling _____.

_____ she _____ tired _____?

_____, she _____.

No, she's _____.

_____ you _____ _____ _____?

Yes, _____ _____.

_____, I'm _____ _____.

_____?

_____.

_____.

th /θ/

3rd

third /θɜrd/

bath /bæθ/

thumb /θʌm/

tooth /tuθ/

More words

three

path

math

thing

thick

Write the words

th /θ/

Write the letters & Read the sentences!

He put his _ _umb in the ba_ _.

He has _ _ree _ _ick ma_ _ books.

The _ _ird pa_ _ is wide.

Complete the words

1. a_____y   3. b_____d   5. e_____c

2. s_____d   4. t_____d   6. f_____d

Write the answer next to the letter "A"

A: ___ **7.** How is he ___?

a. feeling
b. feels
c. felt

A: ___ **8.** How ___ you feeling?

a. is
b. am
c. are

A: ___ **9.** He ___ feeling frustrated.

a. isn't
b. aren't
c. not

A: ___ **10.** Are you feeling tired?

a. Yes, I'm not.
b. Yes, I am.
c. No, I isn't.

Answers on Page 156

- Learn the words
- Learn the sentences
- Learn the phonics
- Test yourself!

At the ice cream shop

в кафе-морозиві

Learn the words

1. **mint**
   м'ята

2. **cherry**
   вишня

3. **strawberry**
   полуниця

4. **chocolate**
   шоколад

5. **raspberry**
   малина

6. **almond**
   мигдаль

7. **coconut**
   кокос

8. **coffee**
   кава

9. **vanilla**
   ваніль

10. **caramel**
    карамель

Write the missing letters!

1. m_ _ _

2. _h_ _r_

3. st_a_b_ _r_

4. c_o_o_ _t_

5. r_ _p_ _r_y

6. a_ _o_ _

7. c_ _o_u_

8. _o_ _e_

9. v_ _i_ _a

10. ca_ _m_ _

Have fun with the words!

Word Search

```
z  c  s  w  q  p  n  r  v  c  h  e  r  r  y  w  g  n
r  o  w  c  s  c  z  q  a  g  z  e  y  m  u  e  a  w
c  f  x  n  h  t  a  j  l  s  s  j  q  u  i  l  d  s
f  f  c  f  d  o  r  r  d  f  p  a  n  q  p  n  w  m
r  e  o  v  w  z  c  a  a  w  a  b  m  h  y  m  t  d
k  e  c  s  a  c  i  o  w  m  q  l  e  q  r  m  x  u
k  u  o  p  a  n  t  r  l  b  e  r  m  r  x  y  p  y
r  b  n  q  t  h  i  x  y  a  e  l  d  o  r  b  r  e
f  g  u  e  n  h  p  l  w  y  t  r  d  m  n  y  g  y
l  i  t  z  n  k  c  f  l  l  u  e  r  h  a  d  y  w
l  v  u  s  d  k  q  d  j  a  o  r  r  y  s  w  d  l
g  h  m  n  v  b  m  l  m  j  q  u  d  q  y  u  m  n
```

Word directions: → ↘ ↓

mint	almond
cherry	coconut
strawberry	coffee
chocolate	vanilla
raspberry	caramel

What's your favorite ice cream flavor?

My favorite ice cream flavor is <u>chocolate</u>.

My favorite ice cream flavor isn't <u>strawberry</u>.

Write the missing words!

What's _____ favorite _____ cream flavor?

My _____ ice _____ flavor is _____.

_____ favorite ice cream _____ _____ vanilla.

_____ his _____ ice cream _____?

His _____ ice _____ flavor _____ _____.

_____ favorite _____ cream _____ isn't _____.

_____ _____ favorite _____ cream _____?

Her _____ ice _____ _____ _____.

_____ favorite _____ _____ flavor isn't _____.

_____?

_____.

_____.

Do you like <u>mint</u> flavor?   Does he like <u>cherry</u> flavor?

Yes, mint flavor is my favorite.   Yes, cherry flavor is my favorite.

No, I don't like mint flavor.   No, he doesn't like cherry flavor.

Write the missing words!

Do you _____ raspberry _____?

Yes, _____ flavor is my _____.

_____, I _____ like raspberry _____.

_____ she like _____ flavor?

_____, almond flavor is _____ favorite.

No, she _____ like _____ flavor.

Does he like coffee flavor?

_____, coffee _____ is _____ favorite.

No, _____ doesn't _____ _____ flavor.

_____?

_____.

_____.

sh /ʃ/

fish /fɪʃ/

ship /ʃɪp/

shoe /ʃu/

shell /ʃel/

More words

brush

sheep

she

shop

shed

Write the words

sh /ʃ/

Write the letters & Read the sentences!

_ _e is bru_ _ing her teeth.

That _ _op has cheap _ _oes.

The _ _eep is in the _ _ed.

Complete the words

1. s_____y   3. c_____e   5. c_____y

2. r_____y   4. v_____a   6. a_____d

Write the answer next to the letter "A"

A: ___ **7.** What's your favorite ice cream flavor?

a. My favorite ice cream is chocolate.
b. His favorite ice cream flavor is mint.
c. My favorite ice cream flavor is cherry.

A: ___ **8.** My favorite ice cream flavor ___ caramel.

a. aren't
b. isn't
c. is'nt

A: ___ **9.** Does she like cherry flavor?

a. Yes, cherry flavor is his favorite.
b. No, she doesn't likes cherry flavor.
c. No, she doesn't like cherry flavor.

A: ___ **10.** Do you like mint flavor? Yes, mint flavor ___ favorite.

a. is my
b. is her
c. is his

Answers on Page 156

Lesson 19

- Learn the words
- Learn the sentences
- Learn the phonics
- Test yourself!

The weather

погода

Learn the words

1. sunny сонячна	**6. cold** холодна
2. rainy дощова	**7. warm** тепла
3. snowy сніжна	**8. hot** жарка
4. cloudy марна	**9. freezing** крижана, морозна
5. windy вітряна	**10. cool** прохолодна

Write the missing letters!

1. s_n_ _   6. c_ _d

2. _a_n_   7. w_ _ _

3. s_ _ _y   8. h_ _

4. c_o_d_   9. f_e_ _in_

5. w_n_ _   10. _ _ o _

Have fun with the words!

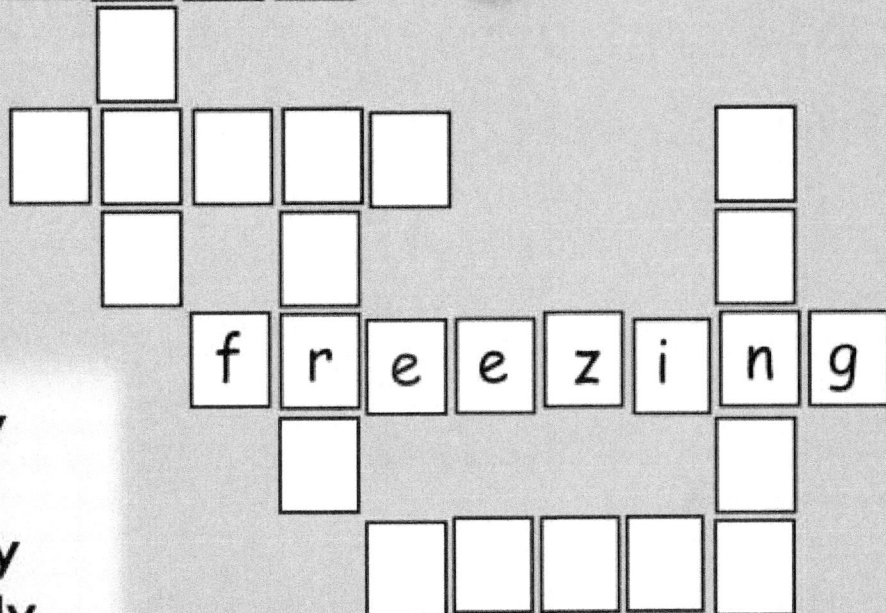

f r e e z i n g

sunny
rainy
snowy
cloudy
windy
cold
warm
hot
freezing
cool

Write the missing word:

How's the weather going to be?

The weather is going to be <u>sunny</u>.

The weather isn't going to be <u>rainy</u>.

Write the missing words!

How's the _____ going _____ be?

The weather _____ _____ to _____ _____.

_____ weather _____ going _____ be _____.

_____ the _____ _____ to _____?

_____ is _____ to be _____.

The _____ isn't _____ _____.

_____ weather _____ be?

_____ _____ going to _____ _____.

The _____ _____ to _____.

_____ ?

_____ .

_____ .

Is the weather going to be <u>hot</u>?

Yes, it's going to be hot.

No, it's not going to be hot.

Write the missing words!

Is _____ weather _____ to _____ _____ ?

Yes, _____ going _____ _____ cloudy.

_____ , it's _____ _____ to be _____ .

_____ the _____ going _____ _____ cool?

Yes, _____ be _____ .

No, _____ not _____ be _____ .

Is _____ going _____ be _____ ?

Yes, _____ _____ to _____ .

_____ , it's _____ _____ windy.

_____ ?

_____ .

_____ .

ch /tʃ/

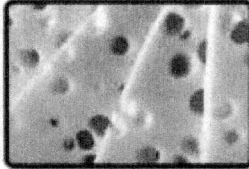

cheese /tʃiz/

chess /tʃɛs/

chick /tʃɪk/

bench /bɛntʃ/

More words

check

chin

cheap

chat

choose

Write the words

ch /tʃ/

Write the letters & Read the sentences!

There is _ _eese on your _ _in.

We sit on the ben_ _ and _ _at.

I will _ _oose the _ _eap _ _air.

Complete the words

1. c_____y   3. f_____g   5. w_____m

2. s_____y   4. r_____y   6. c_____d

Write the answer next to the letter "A"

A: ___ **7.** How's the weather going to be?

a. It's going be freezing.
b. It not going to be cold.
c. It's going to be warm.

A: ___ **8.** It's not ___ be windy.

a. going to
b. go to
c. going too

A: ___ **9.** Is the weather going to be cloudy?

a. No, it not going to be cloudy.
b. Yes, it's going be cloudy.
c. Yes, it's going to be cloudy.

A: ___ **10.** Is ___ going to be hot?

a. weather
b. this weather
c. the weather

Answers on Page 156

Lesson 20
- Learn the words
- Learn the sentences
- Learn the phonics
- Test yourself!

In the living room

в вітальні

Learn the words

1. **coffee table**
журнальний столик

2. **armchair**
крісло

3. **clock**
годинник

4. **television**
телевізор

5. **bookcase**
книжкова шафа

6. **sofa**
диван

7. **vase**
ваза

8. **rug**
килим

9. **TV stand**
підставка під телевізор

10. **painting**
картина

Write the missing letters!

1. _of_ _e t _ _ l_

2. a_ _c_a_r

3. c_ _c_

4. te_e_ _si_n

5. b_ _k_a_e

6. s_ _ _

7. v_ _ _

8. _u_

9. T_ s_a_ _

10. _a_ _t_n_

Have fun with the words!

1. table / front / the / is / of / in / coffee

The sofa _____ .

2. to / stand / TV / next / the / is

The vase _____ .

3. next / the / painting / to / is

The clock _____ .

4. the / in / of / sofa / front / isn't

The bookcase _____ .

5. of / the / in / rug / front / isn't

The painting _____ .

6. isn't / TV / the / stand / to / next

The armchair _____ .

7. in / table / of / coffee / the / is / front

The television _____ .

8. next / the / isn't / vase / to

The rug _____ .

Where is the <u>coffee table</u>?

The coffee table is in front of the <u>TV stand</u>.

It isn't next to the <u>sofa</u>.

Write the missing words!

Where _____ the _____ stand?

The TV _____ is _____ to the _____ .

It _____ in front _____ the _____ .

_____ is _____ table?

The coffee _____ is in _____ of the _____ .

It _____ next _____ .

Where _____ ?

The painting _____ to _____ .

It _____ in _____ the _____ .

_____ ?

_____ .

_____ .

Is the <u>sofa</u> next to the <u>armchair</u>?

Yes, the sofa is.

No, the sofa isn't.

Write the missing words!

Is the _____ table _____ to _____ _____?

Yes, _____ coffee _____ _____.

_____, the _____ _____ isn't.

_____ the painting in _____ of the _____?

Yes, _____ _____ is.

No, _____ painting _____.

Is _____ TV _____ next _____ the _____?

Yes, _____ _____ stand _____.

_____, _____ TV _____ _____.

_____?

_____.

_____.

st /st/

stop /stɒp/

stairs /stɛrz/

star /star/

stamp /stæmp/

More words

stool

store

storm

sting

stove

Write the words

st /st/

Write the letters & Read the sentences!

There is a _ _ar on this _ _amp.

_ _op at this _ _ore and buy a new _ _ove.

Put a _ _ool in front of the _ _airs.

Complete the words

1. c_____k   3. b_____e   5. t_____n

2. a_____r   4. s_____a   6. p_____g

Write the answer next to the letter "A"

A: ___ **7.** Where is the clock?

a. The clock is next of the bookcase.
b. The clock is next to the bookcase.
c. The clock is front of the bookcase.

A: ___ **8.** The vase is in ___ the sofa.

a. front to
b. next to
c. front of

A: ___ **9.** Is the television next to the coffee table?

a. Yes, the coffee table is.
b. Yes, television is.
c. No, the television isn't.

A: ___ **10.** Is ___ in front of the rug?

a. the armchair
b. these armchair
c. armchair

Answers on Page 156

- Learn the words
- Learn the sentences
- Learn the phonics
- Test yourself!

Chores

хатня робота

Learn the words

1. **take out the trash**
виносити сміття

2. **wash the dishes**
мити посуд

3. **feed the pets**
годувати домашніх тварин

4. **vacuum the carpet**
пилососити килим

5. **clean the bedroom**
прибирати в спальні

6. **iron the clothes**
прасувати одяг

7. **mop the floor**
мити підлогу

8. **cook dinner**
готувати обід

9. **do the laundry**
прати

10. **make the beds**
заправляти постіль

Write the missing letters!

1. ta_e o_t th_ t_a_h

2. w_ _h t_e di_h_s

3. _ _ed _he pe_ _

4. v_cu_m t_e c_r_e_

5. cl_ _n th_ b_ _r_om

6. i_o_ t_e c_ot_e_

7. m_p _he f_oo_

8. c_o_d_n_e_

9. d_ t_e l_u_d_y

10. m_ _e _he b_ _s

Have fun with the words!

do • —————————————————————————— • the beds

clean • ————————————————————————— • the laundry

make • • the floor

iron • • the bedroom

mop • • dinner

cook • • the dishes

take out • • the clothes

wash • • the trash

Write the 2 missing chores!

1. _____

2. _____

Which chores do you have to do?

_____

Which chores do you have to do today?

Today, I have to <u>wash the dishes</u>.

I don't have to <u>clean the bedroom</u> today.

Write the missing words!

Which _____ do you _____ to _____ today?

Today, I have _____ take _____ the _____ .

I _____ have to _____ the dishes _____ .

Which chores _____ he have _____ do today?

_____ , he has _____ feed the _____ .

He doesn't _____ to _____ the clothes today.

_____ chores does _____ have _____ do _____ ?

Today, she _____ to do _____ _____ .

She _____ have _____ _____ dinner _____ .

_____ ?

_____ .

_____ .

Do you have to <u>mop the floor</u> today?

Yes, I have to mop the floor.

No, I have to <u>take out the trash</u>.

Write the missing words!

Do you _____ to _____ the carpet _____?

Yes, _____ have _____ vacuum the _____.

_____, I _____ to _____ _____ pets.

Does _____ have _____ clean the _____ today?

_____, she has to _____ _____ bedroom.

No, _____ _____ to _____ the clothes.

_____ he _____ to _____ the beds _____?

Yes, _____ has _____ make _____ _____.

_____, he _____ to _____ _____ dishes.

_____?

_____.

_____.

all /ɔl/

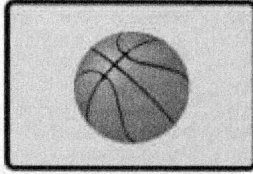

ball /bɔl/

wall /wɔl/

call /kɔl/

stall /stɔl/

More words

all

small

mall

tall

fall

Write the words

all /ɔl/

Write the letters & Read the sentences!

This b_ _ _ is too sm_ _ _.

There is a st_ _ _ in the m_ _ _.

The t_ _ _ man will c_ _ _ you.

Complete the words

1. l_____y

2. c_____t

3. c_____s

4. f_____r

5. b_____m

6. d_____r

Write the answer next to the letter "A"

A: ___ **7.** Which chores ___ you have to ___ today?

a. do, do
b. does
c. is

A: ___ **8.** She ___ make the beds. She ___ to mop the floor.

a. has to, doesn't has
b. have to, doesn't have
c. has to, doesn't have

A: ___ **9.** Does he have to vacuum the carpet today?

a. Yes, he have to vacuum the carpet.
b. No, he has to vacuum the dishes.
c. No, he has to do the laundry.

A: ___ **10.** Does ___ have to feed the pets today?

a. you
b. she
c. they

Answers on Page 156

Pets

домашні тварини

Learn the words

1. **rabbit**
   кролик

2. **cat**
   кіт

3. **dog**
   собака

4. **guinea pig**
   морська свинка

5. **bird**
   пташка

6. **fish**
   рибка

7. **turtle**
   черепаха

8. **mouse**
   мишка

9. **hamster**
   хом'як

10. **snake**
    змія

Write the missing letters!

1. r_ _b_t

2. _a_

3. d_ _

4. g_i_e_ p_ _

5. b_ _d

6. f_s_

7. t_r_l_

8. m_u_e

9. ha_s_ _r

10. s_ _ke

Have fun with the words!

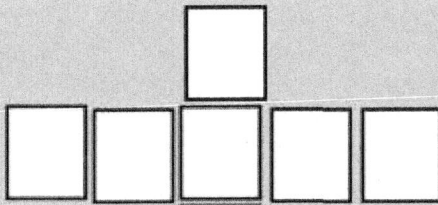

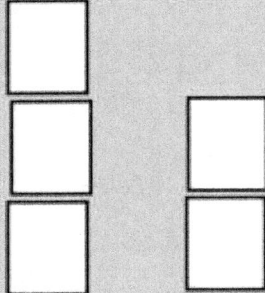

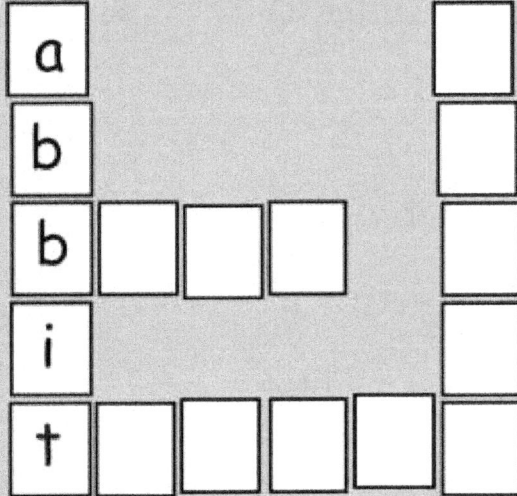

r
a
b
b i t
i
t

hamster
snake
mouse
cat
guinea pig
dog
turtle
fish
rabbit
bird

Write the missing word:

_____

Which pet would you like to get?

I would like to get a <u>hamster</u>.

I wouldn't like to get a <u>snake</u>.

Write the missing words!

Which _____ would you _____ to get?

I _____ like to _____ a _____ .

I wouldn't _____ _____ get _____ fish.

Which pet _____ she like _____ _____ ?

_____ would _____ to _____ a turtle.

She _____ like _____ _____ a _____ .

_____ _____ would they _____ to _____ ?

They _____ like _____ get _____ _____ pig.

_____ wouldn't _____ to _____ a _____ .

_____ ?

_____ .

_____ .

Would you like to get a <u>dog</u>?

Yes, I would like to get a dog.

No, I would like to get a <u>cat</u>.

Write the missing words!

Would you _____ to get _____ fish?

Yes, I _____ like to get a _____ .

No, _____ would _____ to _____ a _____ .

Would they _____ to get a _____ ?

Yes, _____ would like _____ get _____ rabbit.

_____ , they _____ to get a _____ .

Would _____ like _____ get a _____ ?

_____ , he would like _____ _____ a _____ .

No, he _____ _____ _____ get _____ bird.

_____ ?

_____ .

_____ .

ell /ɛl/

bell /bɛl/

well /wɛl/

cell /sɛl/

shell /ʃɛl/

More words

tell

smell

fell

yell

sell

Write the words

ell /ɛl/

Write the letters & Read the sentences!

This sh_ _ _ sm_ _ _s like the beach.

T_ _ _ me why he is y_ _ _ing.

The b_ _ _ f_ _ _ down the w_ _ _.

Complete the words

1. r _____ t   3. s _____ e   5. t _____ e

2. h _____ r   4. m _____ e   6. b _____ d

Write the answer next to the letter "A"

A: ___ **7.** Which pet would you like to get?

a. I would like to get a turtle.
b. I will like to get a hamster.
c. I will like a cat.

A: ___ **8.** She would like ___ a mouse. She ___ like to get a snake.

a. get, wouldnt'
b. to get, wouldn't
c. to get, would'nt

A: ___ **9.** Would he like to get a guinea pig?

a. No, he would like to get a guinea pig.
b. No, he wouldn't like to get a rabbit.
c. No, he would like to get a rabbit.

A: ___ **10.** Would she ___ a fish?

a. likes to get
b. like get to
c. like to get

Answers on Page 156

Lesson 23
- Learn the words
- Learn the sentences
- Learn the phonics
- Test yourself!

Skills

навички

Learn the words

1. swim плавати	**6. cook** готувати
2. ski кататися на лижах	**7. surf** займатися серфінгом
3. sing співати	**8. ride** їхати
4. draw малювати	**9. write** писати
5. read читати	**10. run** бігати

Write the missing letters!

1. s_i_   6. _o_k

2. _k_   7. s_ _f

3. si_ _   8. r_d_

4. d_ _w   9. _ri_e

5. r_ _d   10. r_ _

Have fun with the words!

swim •

surf •

ride •

ski •

run •

Write 4 more skills!

1. _____

2. _____

3. _____

4. _____

What can you do well?

_____

What can you do well?

I can <u>dance</u> very well.

But, I can't <u>sing</u> very well.

Write the missing words!

What _____ you do _____?

I can _____ _____ well.

But, _____ _____ run very _____.

_____ can they _____ well?

They _____ cook very _____.

_____, _____ can't _____ _____ well.

What _____ _____ do _____?

He _____ _____ _____ _____.

_____, he _____ _____ very _____.

_____?

_____.

_____.

Can you <u>surf</u> well?

Yes, I can surf very well.

No, but I can <u>ski</u> very well.

Write the missing words!

Can _____ write _____ ?

Yes, _____ can _____ very _____ .

No, _____ I _____ read _____ well.

_____ she _____ well?

_____ , she can draw _____ well.

No, _____ can _____ very _____ .

_____ you _____ ?

Yes, we _____ swim _____ well.

_____ , but _____ can _____ very _____ .

_____ ?

_____ .

_____ .

ill /ɪl/

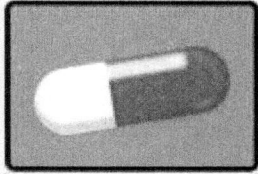

pill /pɪl/

hill /hɪl/

mill /mɪl/

drill /drɪl/

More words

will

still

fill

grill

spill

Write the words

ill /ɪl/

Write the letters & Read the sentences!

The beef is st_ _ _ on the gr_ _ _.

There is a m_ _ _ on the h_ _ _.

I w_ _ _ use my dr_ _ _ to fix the m_ _ _.

Complete the words

1. s_____m   3. r_____d   5. w_____e

2. s_____g   4. c_____k   6. d_____w

Write the answer next to the letter "A"

A: ___ **7.** What can you do ___?

a. goodly
b. good
c. well

A: ___ **8.** He ___ very well. But, he ___ very well.

a. can swims, can't surfs
b. can swim, can't surf
c. can swim, can surf

A: ___ **9.** Can she write well?

a. Yes, she can write very well.
b. Yes, she can writes very well.
c. No, but she can read very good.

A: ___ **10.** Can he ___ well?

a. sings
b. draw
c. wrote

Answers on Page 156

Lesson
24
- Learn the words
- Learn the sentences
- Learn the phonics
- Test yourself!

Meats

м'ясо

Learn the words

1. **beef**
яловичина

2. **fish**
риба

3. **pork**
свинина

4. **salami**
салямі

5. **bacon**
бекон

6. **chicken**
курятина

7. **sausage**
ковбаса

8. **lamb**
баранина

9. **shrimp**
креветки

10. **ham**
шинка

Write the missing letters!

1. b_ _f

2. _i_h

3. _o_k

4. s_l_ _i

5. b_ _ _n

6. c_ _c_en

7. s_ _sa_e

8. l_m_

9. _h_i_p

10. h_ _

Have fun with the words!

Word Search

```
c d u y f t r r l p i f b a p s a e
x m z o r b t w q f u e w a q o x k
m e c h i c k e n a y r r o j x r s
b m b s s k u u i r l j o u s b c k
x a a l a x u s q h a r g r c i r q
x e c m u f x n a q m j z z s x p j
w b o t s p l v b l b j a y h a m y
o w n q a q n h y e a x d m r r n o
g g l l g c x g d n e m n d i k y z
p a e o e a v v v c c f i k m h y k
d x f h h h r f i s h b d p p p z o
l p h x q v y t n n p f f t x h p g
```

Word directions: → ↘ ↓

beef	**chicken**
fish	**sausage**
pork	**lamb**
salami	**shrimp**
bacon	**ham**

What will you be cooking for lunch?

I will be cooking <u>chicken</u> for lunch.

I won't be cooking <u>beef</u>.

Write the missing words!

What _____ you be _____ for _____?

I will _____ cooking pork _____ lunch.

_____ be cooking _____.

_____ will he _____ _____ for lunch?

He _____ be cooking _____ for _____.

_____ won't _____ bacon.

What will _____ cooking _____ _____?

She _____ be _____ shrimp _____ lunch.

She _____ cooking _____.

_____?

_____.

_____.

Will you be cooking <u>fish</u> for lunch?

Yes, I will be.

No, I won't be. I'll be cooking <u>sausage</u>.

Write the missing words!

Will you _____ cooking ham _____ lunch?

Yes, _____ will _____ .

No, I _____ be. _____ be cooking _____ .

_____ she be _____ _____ for _____ ?

Yes, she _____ .

No, _____ won't be. She'll _____ _____ salami.

Will _____ _____ cooking _____ _____ lunch?

_____ , he _____ _____ .

_____ , he _____ be. _____ be _____ _____ .

_____ ?

_____ .

_____ .

ol /oʊl/

roll /roʊl/

old /oʊld/

cold /koʊld/

folder /'foʊldər/

More words

scroll

sold

told

mold

bold

Write the words

ol /oʊl/

Write the letters & Read the sentences!

My father s_ _d the _ _d car.

There is m_ _d on the r_ _l.

I put the scr_ _l in the f_ _der.

Complete the words

1. b_____ f   3. s_____ i   5. b_____ n

2. c_____ n   4. s_____ p   6. s_____ e

Write the answer next to the letter "A"

A: ___ **7.** What will he be eating ___ lunch?

a. for
b. of
c. on

A: ___ **8.** I ___ eating fish for lunch.

a. will been
b. will be
c. won't

A: ___ **9.** Will she be eating beef for lunch?

a. No, she won't be. She'll be eat pork.
b. No, she won't. She'll be eating pork.
c. No, she won't be. She'll be eating pork.

A: ___ **10.** Will they ___ ham for lunch?

a. be eat
b. eating
c. be eating

Answers on Page 156

Lesson 25
- Learn the words
- Learn the sentences
- Learn the phonics
- Test yourself!

Countries

країни

Learn the words

1. **Canada**
Канада

2. **Brazil**
Бразилія

3. **Japan**
Японія

4. **Australia**
Австралія

5. **South Africa**
Південна Африка

6. **Mexico**
Мексика

7. **Germany**
Німеччина

8. **China**
Китай

9. **Russia**
Росія

10. **England**
Англія

Write the missing letters!

1. C_ _a_a

2. B_a_ _l

3. _ap_n

4. A_st_a_ _a

5. S_u_h Af_i_ _

6. _ex_c_

7. G_r_a_y

8. C_i_ _

9. R_ _si_

10. _n_la_d

Have fun with the words!

China •

Australia •

Mexico •

Japan •

Canada •

Brazil •

Germany •

Russia •

England •

South Africa •

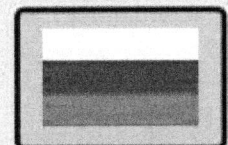

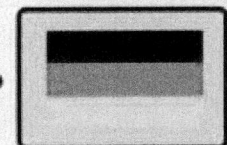

Where will you be traveling to?

We'll be traveling to <u>Canada</u> and <u>Mexico</u>.

We won't be traveling to <u>Brazil</u>.

Write the missing words!

Where _____ you be traveling _____?

We'll be _____ _____ Australia and _____.

We _____ _____ traveling to _____.

_____ will they _____ _____ to?

They'll _____ traveling to _____ _____ Russia.

They _____ be _____ to _____.

Where _____ you _____?

_____ be _____ to _____ and _____.

We _____ be _____ _____ England.

_____?

_____.

_____.

Will they be traveling to <u>China</u>?

Yes, they will be.

No, they won't be. They'll be traveling to <u>Japan</u>.

Write the missing words!

Will they _____ traveling _____ South _____?

Yes, _____ will _____.

No, _____ won't be. They'll be _____ to _____.

_____ you be _____ to Russia?

Yes, we _____ _____.

No, _____ won't be. We'll _____ traveling to _____.

Will _____ be traveling to _____?

_____, they _____ _____.

No, they _____ be. _____ be _____ to _____.

_____?

_____.

_____.

ar /ar/

jar /dʒar/

barn /barn/

shark /ʃark/

star /star/

More words

dark

park

farm

car

arm

Write the words

ar /ar/

Write the letters & Read the sentences!

There is a b_ _n on the f_ _m.

That st_ _ is f_ _.

I hurt my _ _m at the p_ _k.

Complete the words

1. A_____ a   3. M_____ o   5. J_____ n

2. G_____ y   4. E_____ d   6. R_____ a

Write the answer next to the letter "A"

A: ___ **7.** Where will you ___ to?

a. be travel
b. be traveling
c. been traveling

A: ___ **8.** ___ traveling to Mexico and Brazil.

a. They'll
b. They're be
c. They'll be

A: ___ **9.** Will you be traveling to Canada?

a. No, we won't be. We'll be traveling to England.
b. No, we won't. We'll be travel to England.
c. No, we wont'. We'll be traveling to England.

A: ___ **10.** Will they be ___ Japan?

a. traveling
b. traveling to
c. travel to

Answers on Page 156

Answers

Test 1-5	Lesson 1	Lesson 2	Lesson 3	Lesson 4	Lesson 5
Question 1	pencil	computer	yellow	brother	star
Question 2	tape	globe	brown	sister	triangle
Question 3	marker	poster	orange	uncle	octagon
Question 4	eraser	bookshelf	green	aunt	rectangle
Question 5	crayon	whiteboard	black	father	heart
Question 6	whiteout	desk	purple	mother	diamond
Question 7	c	a	b	b	b
Question 8	b	b	c	c	c
Question 9	a	c	a	b	a
Question 10	b	a	b	a	c

Test 6-10	Lesson 6	Lesson 7	Lesson 8	Lesson 9	Lesson 10
Question 1	tiger	builder	strawberry	stomach	tennis
Question 2	bear	nurse	cherry	head	volleyball
Question 3	monkey	salesclerk	watermelon	foot	golf
Question 4	kangaroo	doctor	pineapple	finger	cricket
Question 5	lion	teacher	banana	shoulder	badminton
Question 6	crocodile	chef	lemon	neck	hockey
Question 7	a	B	b	c	a
Question 8	c	c	a	b	c
Question 9	b	b	c	b	a
Question 10	b	a	c	a	b

Test 11-15	Lesson 11	Lesson 12	Lesson 13	Lesson 14	Lesson 15
Question 1	store	blouse	geography	carrot	airplane
Question 2	cinema	sweater	computer	potato	dinosaur
Question 3	park	necktie	history	broccoli	robot
Question 4	restaurant	jacket	music	spinach	teddy bear
Question 5	supermarket	scarf	English	mushroom	ball
Question 6	gym	dress	science	onion	doll
Question 7	b	b	a	b	c
Question 8	b	b	b	c	b
Question 9	c	a	b	a	a
Question 10	a	a	c	c	b

Test 16-20	Lesson 16	Lesson 17	Lesson 18	Lesson 19	Lesson 20
Question 1	blender	angry	strawberry	cloudy	clock
Question 2	stove	sad	raspberry	sunny	armchair
Question 3	pan	bored	chocolate	freezing	bookcase
Question 4	toaster	tired	vanilla	rainy	sofa
Question 5	cupboard	energetic	cherry	warm	television
Question 6	refrigerator	frustrated	almond	cold	painting
Question 7	a	a	c	c	b
Question 8	b	c	b	a	c
Question 9	a	a	c	c	c
Question 10	c	b	a	c	a

Test 21-25	Lesson 21	Lesson 22	Lesson 23	Lesson 24	Lesson 25
Question 1	laundry	rabbit	swim	beef	Australia
Question 2	carpet	hamster	sing	chicken	Germany
Question 3	clothes	snake	read	salami	Mexico
Question 4	floor	mouse	cook	shrimp	England
Question 5	bedroom	turtle	write	bacon	Japan
Question 6	dinner	bird	draw	sausage	Russia
Question 7	a	a	c	a	b
Question 8	c	b	b	b	c
Question 9	c	c	a	c	a
Question 10	b	c	b	c	b

Printed in Great Britain
by Amazon

82030220R00093